Appropriate Detachment

Drew Torchia

Drew Torchia

Appropriate Detachment

ISBN: 9780993760105

Appropriate Publishing

DEDICATION

To my daughter Scarlett

CONTENTS

INTRODUCTION

In modern life there are entirely too many stressors. Many people have trouble making it through their day with their sanity intact. This book is designed as a supplement to whatever form of religion or philosophy that you already practice and enjoy.

With today's modern access to information we have a much more global outlook on the concept of a belief system. This allows us to take pieces from any system of thought and find some benefit from them in our lives. This book is intended as yet another trove of information, tips and fragments of a belief system, that you can opt to incorporate in your life, if you feel you would benefit from them.

Appropriate Detachment allows us, as a people, to be more generally accepting of other people's thoughts and beliefs as we will have gained an understanding of their history and where they come from. Beliefs can be very hard to change and are often a product of our environment. It is only in recent years that there is a spring of people using the power of a global information system to look outside of their own household or neighbourhood for enlightenment.

So please, as you read this book, try to keep an open mind and think about the things in your day-to-day life that bother you and cause stress and try to evaluate if you should give them that much power over you. This book will ask you some tough questions with the goal of having you re-evaluate how you perceive stress and the things that cause you stress, thus arming you to reduce it or in time be free of it entirely.

Read on and enjoy,

1 WHAT IS STRESS?

As cliche as it may be to start off a chapter or a book with a dictionary definition, it is important to understand what it is we are trying to defend ourselves from. "Know thine enemy"

The Oxford English Dictionary defines "stress" as: "A state of mental or emotional strain or tension resulting from adverse or demanding circumstances."

There are myriad definitions for the concept of stress but all focus around the idea of strain, tension or worry being caused by something outside of us. That paints a picture of a person falling victim to stress and being powerless to avoid it.

More often than not stress originates from our own mind; it is our creation and as such we have the power to defeat it. Two people can grow up in similar surroundings then encounter a similar situation and have a completely different reaction to it. A soldier can be deployed in the gravest of circumstances without feeling the quills of stress, yet his friend can have PTSD triggered by simply hearing a story of the soldier's time in combat. We all have our threshold of stress that we can tolerate and it doesn't make us better or worse people, it simply makes us people.

So the key then is to understand stress so that we can systematically work to eliminate the worst effects of it in our lives and by effect live more freely. This book is not here to stand as a testament to the negative effects of stress on a living being — those are palpable. Do a simple internet search and you will find countless cases of just how detrimental stress can be. Its manifestations are not limited to mental well being. Stress can attack your nervous system, create rashes, hives, affect digestion, disturb sleep pattern and of course induce irritability.

Stress can cause you to act, counter to your individual nature. That is the scariest part of all — it clouds your being. Stress can be attributed as a major cause for loss of employment, divorce, depression and general unhappiness.

Let's do a little exercise:

Think about your day to day life. Think about waking up in the morning and trying to plan your day. Getting yourself ready to leave the house and go to work. The commute to work. Think about your work day, bosses, workload, what needs to be done and what deadlines are coming up soon. Think about driving home while planning supper and how you are going to fit everything into your evening. Getting supper ready and making sure you are feeding your family a healthy and positive diet. Think about any of your evening commitments and requirements and about the small slot of downtime that you allow yourself. Now think about getting settled into bed with your mind worrying about how you are going to accomplish all of the following days' challenges.

How was that for you? Did you feel your heart quicken? Did the room get warmer or smaller? Do you now find yourself planning out your next few days? Did this cause you to write out a list? What do these reactions tell us about the physical manifestations of the stress that is embedded in our daily life?

Now for three scary words to say to an adult. Think... About... Money...

What kind of reaction did that stir?

It is no secret, we live high paced, "stressful" lives and they take their toll. We no longer take time for ourselves and we tend to feel that there aren't enough hours in the day. We find ourselves putting off today's work, knowing full-well that tomorrow will have a full day's challenges, all in itself. So here is the ultimate question: Why do we do it?

Why do we stress ourselves out? Why do we place unrealistic expectations on ourselves then get depressed when we cannot achieve them? Why do we quest after a life of unnecessary luxury or impossible appearance when what will bring us happiness is to take the time to experience the life we already have? Does society impose this stress upon us or is it our own creation?

This book does not profess to answer these questions. If someone answers your question for you, you will walk away thinking "wow, they're smart." If someone helps you to answer your own questions you will walk away thinking "what else can I now solve?". This book is meant to arm you with the tools that you need to ease your stress and let go of the things that truly don't matter. No one can tell you what those things are. You must discover them for yourself.

The important thing to take away here is that stress has little to no positive impact on our lives and an impressive detrimental effect. It can really drag us down.

Let's work together to see what we can do about that.

2 WHAT CAN YOU CONTROL?

This question illuminates the central principle of this book and the most important thing you can take away and apply to your life. There are a huge collection of things that are simply not in our control.

Let's walk through a basic example. Imagine yourself driving down an undivided highway at full speed. From your perspective as a driver you have the entire lane to drive in, from the inside of the painted line to the inside of the painted line. Everything that falls in between those lines is yours. An oncoming vehicle will have this same perspective. The paint on the road is around 8 inches wide, there is 8 inches separating you traveling north at highway speed and oncoming traffic traveling south at highway speed. What is there to stop the driver of the oncoming vehicle from having an arm cramp, or sneezing or swatting a fly in his car and swerving 8 inches towards you? That is a real possibility but does that stop you from travelling on the highway? No, because that is something outside of your control.

You can control your position in your lane and give yourself a buffer zone from oncoming traffic. You can stay alert and make sure that you stay in your allotted space and hope that others will do the same. You can do a lot of things to make highway travel a lot safer but you cannot control the actions of the other drivers. With that being said: Why would you focus any of your precious energy worrying about them?

Take a moment to let that sink in. If you are driving and your focus is on your worry or fear of other drivers, will that help them drive more safely? This is a good example of something you cannot control. Not only will your worry and anxiety not improve the skill of other motorists, it will seriously hamper your own reaction time, should something happen on the road. By being so caught up in worry you have actually made the situation less safe.

The interesting part is what happens when we spread this kind of practical thinking to other aspects of our lives, or in time, all aspects of our lives. We start to see all the little places where we are wasting our energy and learn how to refocus it to be more stable and productive people.

The initial skill therefore, is in identifying what is and isn't in your control. There are easy tests to start out with, just ask yourself:

"If I were to drop everything and focus my entire being on this task, would I affect the outcome?"

Let's run through a couple of scenarios where people commonly worry in day to day life and see if this questions fits.

Scenarios

-After writing a test/exam you sit home and worry about what your mark was. You start to plan out all the steps you would have to take if you failed and what impact that would have on your life.

-After applying for a job and sitting in for an interview you go home and worry about whether you will get the job or not. You wonder what that will mean for your life and the well being of your family. You then try to run down if this will be just a job to you or perhaps a career path.

-You have 5 days to go until payday and you still have 3 more bills that need to be paid, however you don't have enough money.

-You have been assigned to take in a lot of new reading, either by work or school and you don't think you can complete it by the prescribed deadline.

-You are wondering if your co-workers/classmates like you.

-You have a sick loved one and you are worried that they might not recover.

-You know someone that is struggling with an aspect of their life and you are worried for them.

-Your neighbour just got a new
Car/TV/Boat/Pool/Bike/BBQ you name it and suddenly the
one you have feels second-rate.

Did some of those hit a little close to home? Could
you relate to them? You are not alone. So many people
spend so much of their precious time and energy on things
they can't hope to make an impact on. This doesn't mean
that you are floating aimlessly through life with no ability to
control your own destiny or path, far from it. This chapter is
about identifying things that you can control, things that you
can make an impact on. That will help you to determine
where to focus your finite energy and time.

Fitness

A big thing that we can control is our physical fitness.
This is also the first thing that most people let slide the
moment stress sinks in. This is not a book dedicated to
fitness so we won't dawdle greatly on how to improve your
fitness but there are a few concepts of fitness that are
important to know.

"Fitness" and "Health" are very different words. What
does that mean? Well, someone whose fitness is considered
elite could be an Olympic athlete or someone completing an
Ironman Triathlon. What they are capable of physically is
beyond impressive but in the process of pushing their bodies
to such extremes, they will invariably have caused a
collection of health issues: Stress fractures, repetitive strain
injuries, pulled and strained muscles, hernias, damaged
vertebrae and depending on their athletic discipline, a host

of broken bones. The same could be said for health, someone who is perfectly healthy is not necessarily below 10% body fat and capable of all sorts of athletic feats. Modern life has advanced us as a species so that we no longer need to be sinewy hunting machines in order to succeed in daily life.

That being said, fitness in moderation, is still a vital part of our lives and it pays dividends in so many other aspects of our being. Someone who does regular, moderate fitness training will be stronger, more resistant to personal injury, more capable of dealing with complex situations and will look more appealing to their preferred mate. There goes four major causes of stress being eliminated in one simple session of fitness. Not to mention the endorphin rush that you get from exercise and the frustration that you can take out on the exercise of your choice. The health benefits are enormous and you will find that as you break through barriers of fitness you will feel more capable of breaking through barriers elsewhere in life.

There are so many different ways to incorporate fitness into your life. Weight training and cardio are not the only ways to a healthier you. Yoga, Pilates, bootcamp, running, hiking, or simply taking the dog for a walk are all great ways to bring a fitness component into your routine. Go out there and find something that works for you and embrace it.

Linking into the next part of your life you have more control over than you may think, the fact that you put in a good workout will make you more inclined to eat more healthily so that you don't contradict all of the hard work you have done.

Health and Nutrition

Let's begin with the same warning as before, this is not a health book (except maybe mental health) and this is not a book about nutrition nor is it a new diet plan. However, most people do worry a great deal about their own health and the health of their loved ones. We also have a tendency to hold a lot of guilt and self-hatred for our bad diets and physical appearance, often preventing us from having a positive outlook on things and valuing ourselves as worthy members of society. This needs to stop. Everyone has the power to change what they eat and their relationship with food. Everyone has the power to choose a healthier lifestyle for themselves and their families even if it starts with a small step. You need to start somewhere.

The most important first step is to know and value the importance of what we are putting in our bodies. You wouldn't build a house with rotten wood, or build a ship with rusty metal, so why do we so frivolously consume things that are essentially poison? With today's access to information through web sites and free documentaries there is only one word to describe someone who doesn't have at least a baseline understanding of nutrition; Ignorant.

There is no escaping the fact that our bodies are built using the nutrients we consume and plagued by the toxins that we pollute ourselves with.

Knowing that basic truth, we should be empowered to research what we are eating and research the benefits and detriments of certain foods and food combinations. The unfortunate fact is that we are also very busy and researching or preparing healthy food is something that most people have deemed lower on their priority list and it often falls to the wayside; replaced by meals of convenience and binges of guilty pleasures.

Health and nutrition is yet another aspect of our lives where a small effort can make a large impact, and the benefits that follow may surprise you. If you are healthier, your body will be more able to fight off disease, allowing you to miss fewer work days. You will feel better and more able, which will give you a more positive outlook on life. Positive thinking is infectious and you may find yourself suddenly inspiring a co-worker or friend to make a change in their lives as well. This effect has the dual benefit of starting them on a good path and ensuring that you remain dedicated to your goals so as not to let them down.

How much food does a human being actually need in a day? The answer may surprise you. We spend a lot of money on food and most of it is over and above what our body needs or can even process in a day. Rather than the food nourishing us, it clogs up our body. So why do we go out of our way to waste money on food that isn't feeding us, but rather is making us sick, fat and miserable. Figure out how much food your body actually needs and feed yourself to promote your health and well being. Do yourself this small favour. You will not regret it.

Sleep

Ah sleep, the enemy to so many people. When you wake up tired, you will have a tendency to stop caring about health and fitness, you might even dread the day ahead. A day of life should be celebrated. Combatting a deficit of sleep can be one of the hardest steps when trying to improve your life but also one of the most rewarding. Completing any step in a life-altering plan will make it so much easier to face the others. Nowhere is that more true than improving your sleep.

If you train hard in terms of fitness, you may find yourself more physically exhausted by the end of the day which will allow you to drift off to sleep more readily and more deeply, therefore leaving you better rested for tomorrow's training session.

Our health and nutrition affects our sleep as well, if we have eaten a balanced diet that doesn't leave us bloated or having heartburn, at the end of the day we will fall asleep more easily. When we are laying in bed we often reflect on our day. If we can look back at a day of good choices and positive nutrition we will feel much less guilty and our minds will be more at ease. The final benefit of a healthy diet is that we will typically not have as much excess body fat, which can be a major cause of sleep defects, from sleep apnoea to basic snoring and sore joints.

The arch nemesis of sleep however is an active mind. When our mind is racing about, we will seldom be able to restfully close our eyes. So the question then becomes, how do we quiet our mind? A still mind is not an easy thing to achieve; however that is the end goal of this book. The journey of self-evaluation of how you interact with the world may take time. There are however some simple steps to get a big head start.

Steps to quiet your mind before sleep:

These are going to sound like age old sayings but there is a reason they have been around for a while.

-Finish today's work today: Don't go to bed with a sink full of dishes assuming that you will do them tomorrow. You may find yourself thinking about those dishes and trying to plan out tomorrow morning so that there will be time to do them. In the time you sat awake and planned that out, the dishes could have been done and you could have slept peacefully. This concept applies to far more than dishes.

-Never go to bed angry: Hopefully in time, with Appropriate Detachment, the threshold of what drives you to anger will be drastically altered, but for the time being if something is making you angry, don't even bother going to bed. If you stay up an extra 2 or even 3 hours to resolve your anger then go to bed with peace of mind, you will still wake up more refreshed. If what is angering you is outside of your control, use other steps in this book to help you let go of it.

-Don't try to sleep until you are tired: You hear so many people complain that there aren't enough hours in the day, but these same people are often spending 45 minutes to a hour in bed before they are tired enough to sleep. If you want to go to bed early, great. Read a book, engage and challenge that beautiful mind of yours. Once you have thoroughly suspended your disbelief and allowed yourself to be transported by the tales of a talented writer, then you should be ready for sleep. Once you have dropped your book on your lap four or five times and read the same line three times as your eyes get heavy, you are ready. You will find that the quality of your sleep will make up for the time lost reading and you will wake up feeling more rested.

-Take care of yourself: When you lie in bed and turn off your light, it is inevitable that your mind will think back on the events of the day. If you have made good choices: worked out, eaten healthy food, accomplished a goal or task and you are truly tired from a full day of life, you will find that your mind rests more easily. You are well on your way to being able to quiet your active thoughts and just be.

Choosing who you share your life with

This step can be complex and is not for the faint of heart. This section could indeed be a book unto itself but let's just quickly touch on this. There are several categories of people that you have in your life, in this case divided into spheres. We will talk about the work sphere, family sphere, friend sphere and love sphere. Let's briefly cover each of these, going over some basic areas that you do have control over.

Family Sphere

This refers more to the family you are born into and marry into and less about the family that you have made for yourself (wife/husband and children if you have any). This is the sphere that we have the least control and least amount of choice about. Although you have some choice over the family you marry into, you are born into a certain household and that extended family may cause a certain amount of stress. What you can do here is pick your battles. You can focus on your interactions with family and ensure that you don't instigate any arguments, doing your utmost to resolve any ill will. Accept your family for who they are and consider your audience when dealing with them. This will not be an easy task and will often involve swallowing your pride but a stressful situation coming from family will be able to get past your armour more than any other, so be wary.

Work Sphere

In terms of order of control, this sphere is next above family. You do, however, have the power to change jobs or indeed change whole fields of work. If you are in a career that you love but you work with people that cause you stress, this can be a difficult situation. Your control level over this sphere is somewhat dependent on your field of employment. You can choose your business partners or ask for a transfer if you are in a stressful work place. You also have the option of reporting any harassing behaviour to a supervisor to ease the stress of your current situation. We spend quite a bit of time at work every day, so it is important to find something that you enjoy doing.

Friend Sphere

Here is an example of something you have a lot of control over. Some people are still friends with the clique with whom they attended high school, but this is far from the norm. Often people meet friends through work or social activities. Once you are married, you may find new friends in the significant others of your spouse's friends. Once you have children, you will find yourself spending time with the parents of your children's friends or team-mates.

You do however, have a lot of control over who you choose to spend your time with. Associating yourself with like minded people who have similar hobbies will go a long way to helping you maximize your down time. Getting the most out of your social time ensures that you are not wasting hours of precious time with people that either don't help your stress level or exacerbate it.

Love Sphere

Love is the area that can cause the most stress and conversely, can be the area that alleviates the most stress. It all depends on the strength of your connection. You have supreme control over who you spend your life with and while you may feel pressure one way or the other, there is no rush to be paired up by a certain age. When choosing a life mate you should consider that you must look beyond mere sexual desirability. You will be sharing every road trip with this person, every night on the couch, every holiday and vacation, every meal. You will be spending an inordinate amount of time together, so you had better at least get along. You don't just need to get along with each other, you both should get along with each other's family, and your families should get along at least enough to make nice at events. This pursuit can make for quite a search and can seem fairly picky but in the end it will take away a huge amount of strain and stress if you can find someone that satisfies some or most of this criteria.

This text is not a relationship book or a guide to finding that "special someone" but it's only fair to cover a couple of basic tips. If you are unhappy with or in a fight with your significant other, that can leave you feeling like you have nowhere to turn. The most important thing in any relationship is communication. Try to talk about any problems while they are still small, otherwise they will grow to be bigger than the two of you. You may find yourself shouting at someone for stacking the dishes wrong on the drying rack. That wasn't why you were mad. If it is a touchy subject to bring up, try writing a text or email them, that way you have time to plan out what you want to say and make sure that the wording is clear. Appropriate Detachment's applications towards relationship advice could be a book in itself but what is clear is that if you are less stressed, you will bring less outside stress into your relationship. You will be more capable of dealing with whatever may come up in your relationship and strengthen it by your ability to be calm.

Work and Budget

These two items don't immediately seem like they fall

under the same category but the overall stressor here is money. There is an aspect of job satisfaction here but that is always weighed against money. We can work a job that we really love and be happy on a lot less money, whereas if we hate our job, we had better be getting paid well for it. So the question comes down to: "Do we make enough money to satisfy what we deem to be our needs?" It may amaze you just how little money we actually need to get by on. Any extra money gets prioritized according to our own personal appetites and interests. There are self-improvement books in a lot of fields, budgetary planning and job satisfaction is yet another field that this book will not cover in detail, except to state that we have the power in our minds to decide if we make enough money. Alternately, regardless of how much we make, with the wrong mindset it will never be enough.

Down Time

We lead very busy lives, so it becomes increasingly important to step away from our rushed schedule at regular intervals and let our mind focus on something different or simply shut down for a while and reboot. Find a hobby that is within your price range and offers you something that you enjoy.

Our modern world has so many choices in terms of entertainment and escape. You have options ranging from books and literature to comics and magazines, from TV and movies to computer work and video games, from playing sports to watching sports, from crafts to art work. You name it and there is a host of websites dedicated to it. There are groups and communities of people that are there to share in any interest you may have.

Finding people with common interests will help you make a connection, but don't be shy to do an activity on your own if you prefer. If you have a social job it can be nice to have some alone time. The most important thing is to find a hobby or multiple hobbies that you enjoy and that provide you with catharsis. Our hobbies should support the rest of our lives not consume them — some hobbies have a slippery slope towards obsession. The key here is moderation, we have the power to control and balance our time and mental energy across these hobbies. It is up to us to assess which hobbies are helping us relieve stress and which ones are adding to our stress level.

Knowledge of Computers (keeping up with the times)

Here is the most important computer tip you will ever receive: They are not going away.

If your job at all involves you using a computer, it behoves you to take at least a remedial or introductory course on how to use them. In many cases your employer may even pay for the course and give you the needed time off to complete it. So much of many people's work stress revolves around issues with navigating computer menus, lost files, or inefficient use of time on a computer, which leads to missed deadlines and even more stress.

If you are a teacher, you would be best served by learning to create detailed spreadsheets to track your students marks. When report cards are due, you don't have to go back and review a full semester's work, you simply refer to the running totals in your spreadsheet.

If you are a manager you should be capable of keeping detailed files and folders, tracking your employees' performance and correspondence. This allows you to readily evaluate their performance and assign rewards to better motivate your staff.

In any field of work you should be able to produce concise and correct emails and correspondence within an exacting format and learn how to create templates to make your work faster.

If you are a musician you should learn about the many ways to record and master music on a personal computer. You should be comfortable with how to get your music out to the masses and promote it. You should be able to coordinate with people that can help you create compelling online videos for your music, to drum up interest.

If you have children you should be able to set up parental controls and lockout passwords so that you can trust your kids on a computer. You should be able to teach them how to use a computer, not the other way around.

Being able to use a computer, phone, tablet, you name it, will keep you in touch with the flow of modern technology as it progresses, making our lives easier and more powerful.

If you ignore the changing times and let technology get away from you it will become a constant source of frustration and stress to do simple, mundane computer tasks.

Conclusion

There are many things in this life that we cannot control, but we are not helplessly floating through life. This chapter holds examples of things we can control but it is by no means a definitive list. We are powerful beings made more-so by the advent of modern technology and its access to information. You are doing yourself a disservice if you don't take control of the things you can in your life.

The key then, is to be able to discern what is within our control and what isn't. This will allow us to focus our finite energy towards tasks that have a realistic solution. In the next chapter you will learn about the titular concept of this book, Appropriate Detachment and how that will help us, once we have discovered something in our life that is outside of our control.

3 WHAT IS APPROPRIATE DETACHMENT?

We have been through a couple of opening chapters together and now you are ready for the core-concept of this written work. You may find that this concept is disarmingly simple and that is the idea. Do not however, assume that its simplicity makes it any easier to learn or master. This concept will allow you to make small initial changes in your life but in time as you learn, you will get closer and closer to mastering this ability and living stress free. Here is the basics of it spelled out as clearly as possible.

-Analyze your life or an aspect of it and find something that is outside of your control. (this refers to something that is completely out of your hands, so that no conceivable action on your part will have any bearing on the outcome.)

-Instead of worrying about that aspect, or planning for it, or making lists to compensate for possible outcomes, just simply let it go. Erase that item from your mind. You can do nothing to effect its outcome, so do nothing. This frees up your mind to tackle the jumble of remaining tasks that you have to complete.

-So once again: Identify something that you cannot control, and just let it go.

Pros and Cons of Worry?

Appropriate Detachment is much easier said than done. We are all so focused on our worry that we don't stop to think about what effect that worry has on our lives. Has worrying about something ever had a positive effect on its outcome?

Really think about that. Can you name a time that something was out of your control but then you started to worry about it and that worry fixed it all up? Probably not.

So if worrying doesn't do anything to accomplish the myriad tasks that are out of our control, why do we do it?

We have landed on the ultimate question. Most of the time we can't help ourselves or so it seems. We have grown up surrounded by so much worry that it appears like a natural part of our lives. Worry is so ingrained in our daily lives that we assume it to be mandatory.

At this point it is important to clarify the difference between the use of the word "worry" in this book and the concept of "concern". Worrying in this case refers to the grumbling in your mind about all the things you need to get to, the psychological version of running in place. By no means are you being discouraged from being concerned about other people or even yourself. Compassion and empathy are the building blocks of understanding. Unless you can put yourself in someone's shoes, you can't hope to learn anything from their life.

The theme of this book identifies that worry does not contribute to solving these problems, in fact, it robs your mind of free time and brain function. This newfound time and brain function can be used to complete tasks that you can now get to, thereby easing the pressure of further stress and combatting its vicious cycle. This small step can quite literally save you from a collection of stress related sicknesses and drastically improve your productivity while stabilizing your mood and emotional state.

Sounds like a win/win, but no one will tell you it's an easy thing to do. Simply letting go can be just as scary as worrying but with practice and reasonable expectations you will be well on your way to worrying less and doing more.

So let's do the subchapter heading justice, what are the CONS to worrying?

-Worrying about anything at all is guaranteed to spike our stress levels.

-Worrying doesn't actually accomplish the task at hand.

-Worrying uses up valuable time that can be assigned

to another task that we can actually accomplish.

-Worrying eats up much needed brain power that has a far more efficient use.

-Worrying drags others down with us, as people often voice their worries to a companion.

-Worrying focuses on the "what if?" questions which rarely lead to useful solutions.

What about the PROS?

-Specific to the security field (IT or physical) "What if?" questions and worrying about possible modes of ingress into a secure system or building can be vital to your work.

-A quick session of "What if?" can help us determine if problem has an avenue that we can still impact but once something is deemed outside of control the "what if?" questions should stop.

So we can very quickly see that the CONS of worry far outweigh the PROS. If you catch yourself worrying about something, take a deep breath and occupy your mind with something immediate that you have influence over. This idea ties in nicely with the next subchapter, the importance of knowing our enemy.

We have met the enemy and his name is "What If?"

This subchapter shows you a great way to catch

yourself when you start to spiral down a path of worry. You will inevitably find yourself asking questions that begin with "What If?". There is no end to the "What If?" line of questioning; It is like a small child asking "Why?". No matter how many times you answer it, the question "Why?" will still be valid.

If you are having trouble figuring out if you still have some aspect of control over something, it may be of benefit to ask yourself a couple of quick "What If?" questions. You will learn over time how many is enough and it will be case dependent. When you find yourself making lists of "What If?" scenarios or asking the question time and again, it will become clear that this is something you should probably just let go of.

This process will get easier the more you do it and in fact at first it may seem more stressful to let something go rather than to focus on it. This too shall pass, and you will soon discover just how much of your time and energy you were devoting to answering mental "What If?" questions and worrying about their outcomes.

Why "Appropriate Detachment"?
Why use the term "Appropriate Detachment" and what does it mean?

The goal here is to let go of things that we cannot control and are dragging us down.

This idea incorporates isolating or detaching yourself

from those things. They don't necessarily need to be dead to you but you need to be able to fully put them out of your mind, unless something changes that puts control over them back in your hands. Now we can't go around and detach ourselves from everything. We can't fully detach from our work, our kids or our problems — life doesn't allow for that. So the core principle then becomes deciding when it is appropriate to detach ourselves from an item in our life. Hence: Appropriate Detachment.

This way of life can be an art form, so don't expect to be a master right out of the gate. There will be stumbling blocks along the way. You may be scared at first to let certain things go. We have lived our lives a certain way for so long that it seems impossible to imagine anything else. At some point you may even take it too far and step away from something that you still had some sway on, that can have consequences as well. So why bother?

Imagine yourself as an efficient person, focussing maximal effort on aspects of your life that you have maximal impact on. Assigning priorities to the other aspects of your life based on how much sway you have over them, tapering down to the items that you cannot control. Imagine being able to truly not concern yourself with those items, freeing up your full potential to focus on attainable goals.

A few stumbling blocks along the way are worth it to get anywhere closer to an imagined perfect version of our efficient selves. There may be an enormous sliding scale between where you find yourself now and that person, but day by day you will make progress and see the results of your improvement.

Emotion Control

Many people are slaves to their own emotions. Our emotions can help us to inform our choices but they can also blind us. Consider this:

-Have you ever heard of a "blind rage"?

Of course you have, who hasn't?

-Have you ever heard of a "blind calm"?

Of course not, that is just silly.

-So why do we choose to live our lives blind?

This lesson is passed on in, of all things, competitive martial arts. So if, in such a seemingly violent avenue, rage is not a welcome emotion, why should it have any value in our households or workplaces?

Think about all of the decisions that we have to make on a daily basis; not just the big stuff like who to promote or which car to buy. The mundane and the grand, every choice has a massive impact on our lives and creates ripples of consequence that precede us in everything we do.

You could be running late on your way to a job interview and see someone whose car has broken down on the side of the road. You stop to provide them help potentially missing your interview time, only to discover that the person needing help is your interviewer.

You could decide that today you don't want your home brewed coffee but instead go to a local coffee shop near your work, leaving early to make time. While there, you bump into someone who, in time, becomes a life long friend or spouse.

You could do something as mundane as taking a day off work because you are feeling ill and that is the day that your building catches fire, trapping people inside.

Think back on your life. Think about when you met someone important to you. Think about all of the little details that had to line up in order for you to meet in just the way you did. It can be quite humbling.

For this reason you must never make a decision lightly and never without your full faculties present.

Have you ever written an email or letter and before sending it, taken the time to read it over, aloud? You may read it back wondering, what you were trying to say, even though you wrote it only 5 minutes before. This is because by reading it aloud you are using different parts of your brain then when you wrote it. It is as if a completely separate person is reviewing it. Imagine if you had the foresight to be able to look at your daily decisions that way. The goal is to step outside of you and evaluate the bigger picture before acting. Imagine what you could accomplish.

The only way to step outside of our mind and look at

the bigger picture is to dampen the sway that our emotions have on our decision-making. Our emotions trap us within ourselves and prevent us from seeing the whole. It will not be an easy journey to avoid them but it is possible. This idea leads again to the concept of detachment — our emotions still exist but we merely step away from them for a moment to have a clear mind in order to decide what to do.

Time for a very important distinction: when we bottle up our emotions they will come back to haunt us. You may find your body taking the brunt of it, your shoulders will cramp up and your neck will be tense. What we are talking about here is to acknowledge our emotions, then take a step away from them to make a choice with a clear mind. You may find, eventually, you spend less and less time with many of your emotions. They are never gone but they inform us, rather than control us.

Empty Cup

As before these topics lead nicely from one to the next, forming a cohesive system of thought. The next aspect of which is the idea of the empty cup.

There is an age-old teaching of a master offering tea to a student. Upon the student's polite acceptance, the master starts to pour tea into the student's cup. He keeps pouring and pouring until the student's cup overflows and spills on the table. The student is terrified to say anything but finally speaks up and politely asks his master to stop pouring. The master explains that when your cup is full, it can no longer accept any new tea.

The lesson here is about having an open mind. If we walk around this amazing world of ours assuming that we know everything, our minds won't have any room to learn anything new.

Drink from the cup of life and absorb its teachings, then you will always have room in your cup to learn new things. We must be open to new ideas.

Ideas get spoiled over time and memories fade, so if you decide, right now, that you have learned everything that you want to learn, then the only possible outcome is regression.

This concept fits in well with Appropriate Detachment as it's only with a clear mind that we can truly evaluate something new. If we compare it to what we know before and how we feel about that emotionally then we pollute this new idea with our own past.

Over time you may opt to detach yourself from the power that your emotions and your past holds over your decision-making and simply live in the moment. This is not a suggestion to ignore the lessons of history (the world's or your own) but rather to step outside of yourself and view the whole situation. Look at what led you up to this moment and attempt to assess where this choice will lead you. In time you may feel yourself being led in certain areas, don't fight this, as they say, "go with the flow".

Detaching yourself from your ego

Think of your ego as a passenger inside your body, someone you bring with you throughout every minute of every day. It is the voice in your head, your conscience, your guilt and all of your self-imposed rules wrapped into a narcissistic attention hog. The one thing your ego is not, is your ally.

Your ego can conceal itself as "informed thought", or as a sounding board to process information, but don't be fooled. The outcomes that you and your ego plan out together won't always work out as well in the real world.

How then do we avoid being overly influenced by our egos? It is important once again to avoid bottling things up. Your ego exists and it isn't going away. For some, it is a voice telling them that they are a shining star and in doing so it looks down on everyone else. For others, their ego constantly tries to tell them they can't accomplish anything and beats them down. If you simply pretend that this voice in your head doesn't exist, it may resort to becoming louder and stronger in order to be heard once again.

Following the same approach that we took to steel ourselves from our emotions will also work against your ego. Acknowledge that your ego exists and that it has an opinion, then take that same step away and look outside yourself for the true answer.

How do we do that? When you need a sounding board, use another human being. Preferably use someone completely outside of the situation. An outside eye often gives you an unbiased perspective that can be very hard to come up with on your own.

When you have to make an important choice, think about the good of the whole. If you stop living your life purely to benefit yourself and start to elevate other people, you will find yourself in a world of more evolved, less stressed out people.

What words do you associate with someone who overly values the opinions of their own ego? Egomaniac, Narcissist, Selfish, Braggart, the list goes on. It stands to reason then that if you detach yourself from the opinions of your ego you will qualify for such terms as: compassionate, selfless, humble, honest, team-player and nice.

Who would you rather be?

Which set of people do you think has happier, less stressed out lives?

Conclusion

So, the idea of Appropriate Detachment is both disarmingly simple and deceivingly complex at the same time. You merely step outside of your emotions and your situation to make decisions, remembering that all choices are important. More so, if you have identified something that your choices will not impact, you simply let it go. Step away and let your mind focus on more pressing matters that you can actually influence.

At this moment you probably feel intrigued but more

than a little scared or lost. That is fine, we will walk through this together and get you started on a journey that will hopefully bring more balance to your life.

4 THE FREEDOM OF LETTING GO

Every day we run into people that are having a bad day, or an off day, or a bad hair day or even a "case of the Mondays". We run into people who have chosen to not enjoy the whole rest of their day of life, due to the most innocuous of problems.

-The barista only put one sugar in their coffee, instead of two.

-They woke up late.

-Their hair won't cooperate today.

-They stubbed their toe.

-They got a flat tire.

-They're sleepy.

-They forgot their lunch.

At 40 years old you will have spent 14,600 days alive. What percentage of those did you waste because you decided to be miserable for something as mundane as these examples? What new wonders could you have learned, on those days, if you had been in good spirits and open to the idea of some new discovery? Enough about lost time, let's focus on your future and how we can evolve beyond this problem.

Imagine a more efficient you

Imagine a more efficient self. A you who can brush off the small annoyances of life, knowing that, in the bigger picture, they are only as powerful as you allow them to be. Imagine never having a bad day or never losing your temper. What does it really accomplish? Losing your cool alienates loved ones and makes people less willing to bring you new ideas. You have then not only ruined today but you've closed the door on so many future possibilities.

Imagine if you could go through life with a suit of emotional armour, but without bottling anything up. Your emotions still exist but you don't give them a voice in your decision making process.

Imagine being able to shut your mind off before bed and truly rest at night. No tossing and turning, worrying about things that you either have no power over or don't really affect you in any way.

Imagine being able to sit quietly in a room, with your mind at peace. Just being able to shut down and absorb your environment.

Imagine keeping your body in a state of balance, where you are happy with how you look and feel. You would minimize your health risks by living a healthy lifestyle and staying away from stress.

Imagine keeping your life in a state of balance, spending the right amount of time at work, with your family and in personal hobbies and down time.

Imagine being surrounded by people that will help you improve and finding that significant other with whom you can truly be yourself.

Imagine being able to accomplish more at work in a given amount of time than ever before, because you can now focus a larger portion of your mind to the task at hand.

Imagine going through life without worry.

Possibilities

All of these ideal selves are attainable, but getting there won't be easy and everyone will progress at different speeds. Don't expect to transition from a stress case to the Zen master in the time it takes you to read one book. The key here is to improve our lives. That improvement can be incremental at first but as you get better at the basic concepts and learn to apply them to a broader set of challenges, you will be amazed what you can accomplish.

If you set realistic expectations for yourself and

understand that change takes time, you will get far greater enjoyment and value out of the teachings of this book. Try not to get stressed out by the fact that you are struggling to not stress out. It can happen.

Think about how long you have been living your life as you do now. If in six months you can begin to break the cycle and start to make an impact in the way you receive new ideas and you learn to better focus your energy, you are doing great.

Once you get going, it is amazing how the momentum picks up, it will get easier and easier. It may seem like a daunting task but you will get there. Your end line doesn't have to be the sort of Zen Master state. If you are at least somewhat less stressed and driven by emotion, consider your efforts a raging success.

How does this fit in with my current belief system?

This too can be frightening. Initially Appropriate Detachment may seem like a complete belief system in and of itself. While this concept has its roots in eastern religions like Taoism, Buddhism and Zen it should in no way interfere with your chosen religion. We live in a global community now and it behoves us to be more accepting and understanding of foreign concepts. Use the wisdom of the world to inform your daily life. Stand on the shoulders of giants and drink from the pages of world history.

Regardless of your current religious or philosophical

beliefs you can get some value out of the teachings of this book. The beauty is that you can choose how far to follow these ideas. If this book brings up no conflicting ideologies, then you are free to fully lose yourself in the quest for emotional balance and Appropriate Detachment. If you have some more stringent current beliefs then you can at least take the edge off of your stress level, using some of the basic techniques.

Try not to add stress to your life by being overly concerned with whether or not you are being faithful to your current belief system — that would defeat the purpose.

Letting go can be scary at first

Depending on your beliefs and background, you may have spent your whole life addicted to worry. In some belief systems the concept of detachment exists but relies on you leaving these choices up to a "higher power" of sorts. You are then left to pray to that "higher power" in order to help your problems along. The concept of taking a step back from that and really just letting them go can be scary. You may even find yourself feeling kind of exposed just because it is so different from what you are used to.

In time it will get easier and easier to let go of certain things. In fact, once you get comfortable with the concept you may find it difficult not to brag about how freeing it is. It may even be hard right now, to imagine yourself not worrying about these sorts of things, it can be such a foreign concept.

We all grow up with viewpoints that have been passed on to us. Looking for wisdom elsewhere does not mean that we are accusing those viewpoints of being wrong or lacking. Your ideas and ideals evolve over time based on our surroundings. Our surroundings are no longer limited to our immediate area. The Internet has opened the world to us. We are now influenced by the cultures of the world and, in many ways; we can influence the cultures of the world.

So why do it?

This may seem like a scary process with a payoff that may take years, so why bother? Why do it at all? This will be a choice that each and every one of you will have to make but the concept of self-help or self-improvement is real and important. We, as a people, need to keep progressing and getting better and more tolerant or the thin veil of society will crumble around us.

Especially in cities and countries that are a little more multinational, everyone who lives there brings with them their own culture and belief system. If we don't have an open mind, or are not accepting of other people's views, then we will continually be fighting an uphill battle. Too quickly we assign a word to someone we have met. Some one-word throwaway term suggesting that they are different than us, and therefore we don't have to respect them or care about them. In some cases we even use that word to justify a hatred of them. This word can be "selfish" or "arrogant" it can be the name of a race or religion they practice. It can be their job or class, the list goes on. People see a heavily muscled man and say "steroids" or see a slim woman and mutter "anorexic" or "go eat a sandwich".

Too often, we associate someone with one of these terms, then just dismiss them as a human being. "I know I made a mess on the floor of the theatre but there are people they pay to clean that", "I know I poured sticky jam all over the table but that is part of the waitress' job", "don't concern yourself with him, he is kind of a jerk anyways" or "Ignore them, they are (insert race and or religious derogatory term here)". Reading these phrases on a piece of paper we know that they are wrong but we are often guilty of similar attitudes, albeit maybe a little more subdued than some of these examples.

If you are less stressed, more relaxed, well rested and you have an open mind, ready to learn new things, you will find that you get so much more out of interacting with people. You gain an insight into their lives and can therefore really bond with them on a more meaningful level. It will also help you to identify some of these negative qualities in your own personality and force you to evaluate how you interact with people around you. In doing so, you will find it easier to make friends, often friends from varying backgrounds, which broadens your understanding of the world we live in.

It is difficult to comprehensively list the benefits of this way of life, because they manifest themselves in every fiber of your being. If you can let go of the things that clog up your mind, day in and day out, it will grant you extra brainpower, time and residual energy. That energy and time can be focused towards bettering yourself in terms of fitness and healthy eating, which (let's be honest) go hand in hand. The energy you expend at a gym or outdoors will be returned to you with interest when you take on your next task.

This principle snowballs until you find the ideal you. Someone who is physically fit and eats healthy therefore has a lot of residual energy. Someone who has studied the cultures of the world, yet keeps their mind open so they can learn from every conversation and from every new person they meet. Someone who isn't plagued by worry or fraught with stress about things they have no control over.

You may not even be able to picture yourself as this person, depending on your starting point, but you can get there. At the very least you can get a lot closer to there, than where you are now, and improvement is the name of the game.

Conclusion

This chapter touched on some of the freedom that you will gain by progressively learning to let go of worry and opening your mind to new things. Spending less time judging and worrying about other people or the possible outcomes that have very little impact on your life frees up your time to focus on things like your own health. Being healthy and knowing that you take care of yourself leads to a much more peaceful state of mind and a larger overall energy pool.

One thing leads to another and anything you do to improve your body and mind will benefit your life and lead to further research into things that will better you as a whole. Start your upward, positive trajectory now.

5 HOW DO YOU LET GO?

We now come to, in a way, the ultimate question. This book asks a lot of questions to you and forces you to look at some aspects of your life and attitude that might be uncomfortable at first. It's about time you got to ask a fair question in return. How do you do it? The basic concept is clear enough but what about the technicals? How is Appropriate Detachment actually done?

There isn't one simple answer that will apply to everything for everyone. The best solutions vary case by case, person by person, or item by item slated to be detached. We will go over a couple of options for how to let things go, or shut them out but this is by no means a comprehensive list.

Let's start with the simplest and most accessible concept, logical reasoning.

Logical Reasoning

Logic is a very powerful way to step outside of an equation and observe your situation with a fresh pair of eyes. Logic is not without its flaws. A great line comes up.

"All logic in inherently flawed because it is under the assumption that you are not making any assumptions."

That being said, logic is still a great tool to look at the bigger picture. This might be best explained with yet another example. This time we will work with a powerful source of stress for many people, air travel. Let's walk through the process together.

You deal with the hassle of packing and finding someone to look after your pets and you get to the airport. You clear security and finally find your gate. Hopefully you have left decently early so you have a moment to secure some food and a drink of some kind. For the sake of the story let's say the flight leaves at noon and it is 11:00 AM. You find yourself a seat to wait. Now and again you will hear various announcements about your flight but other than that you have very few responsibilities at this time. Revel in that idea. Use this time for a Sudoku puzzle, Crossword, nice book, comic book, rest your eyes, whatever helps you decompress. This is your time.

Most people's mistake comes at pre-boarding. Air travel itself is such a rushed event where you feel there is so much hanging on your shoulders. Depending on how you pack, there may actually be a lot on your shoulders. The airline makes a pre-boarding announcement, usually asking for young families, people needing extra help and the first few rows that opted to spend the extra money. At this time you will find that 60-70% of all passengers will get up from their comfortable seats and start to meander towards the terminal. This clogs up the space for people that need to get through and for the staff that need access. But for you as the passenger this means you leave the comfort of your seat and have to shoulder your bags only to wait in a gaggle that isn't yet being processed. Even when they call for passengers in your rows there is often a line-up that begins beyond the seating area. Therefore, most people get up, walk away from their seat, through the terminal to get in a line up that will eventually proceed past the chair that they were just in. Not to mention if you are in an aisle seat and you get on board before the middle or window seat passenger, then you will have to get up again to let them in before you can get settled.

What is the alternative? You are all going to the same place, you all have a ticket to fly and you all have an assigned seat. Where possible, and once the novelty of the window seat has worn off (often 3 flights), book yourself for an aisle seat. With the exception of when the drink cart comes through, that will give you extra space to stretch out one leg and one arm. This also assures that you won't disturb people by boarding a little later or going to the bathroom. When the rows are being called and people are lining up, stay in your comfortable chair in the terminal. You getting up and getting in line right now is not going to make the plane leave any sooner. You are much more relaxed and you have more space in the terminal so if you have to wait either way, let it be there.

Armed with this new approach you may also want to start booking yourself as close to the front of the plane as possible. You control when you board a plane, you decide when you should get up from that chair and join in the gaggle headed for the terminal. When the plane lands however, passengers get out from the front to the back. Being the last one on and the first one off ensures that your wait time is spent outside of the plane, as much as possible.

Let's say you are near the back of the plane getting off. Once the plane stops everyone stands up and has that crooked back, angled neck thing going on. While it is a nice look, it is not the most comfortable configuration. Know where your bag is and be able to lunge for it when possible but otherwise, stay right in your seat. Keep reading that book or doing that puzzle until the passengers three or four rows in front of you are deplaning. Then gather your things, well rested and get off the plane.

These little tweaks seem simple but they require time to figure out and most of all they require people-watching. But once you have the information all it takes is a bit of logic to work it out and it makes a big difference while traveling.

So remember:

-You have no control over the time the plane takes off and you have an assigned seat. As long as you are in that seat before the plane leaves, it will leave with you.

-When deplaning be near the front of the plane, if not stay in your seat and relax until passengers three rows up grab their gear.

-Find your gate first then check your timing, that way you know just how long you have to shop or get food.

-Always have a book or puzzles or whatever you do to decompress handy so you can maximize your downtime.

Air travel is just one example of a situation that can be completely overhauled using the concept of logical reasoning and Appropriate Detachment. It affords you the ability to step outside of your role as the observer and look at the bigger picture. With an outside view, a detached view, it becomes much easier to analyze the best course of action. In early stages, don't be shy to ask an outside observer for help. Find someone completely removed from the situation and run the particulars by them, they will help you to reach a true solution to the problem. Our own association with any situation clouds our judgment. Learn to detach yourself from situations and observe them using logical reasoning. You will be amazed at how much of your life can be streamlined.

People-Watching

People-watching is a vital part of Appropriate Detachment. Whenever you are in a public or semi-public place there is the opportunity to learn from other people.

You can learn just as easily, what works and what doesn't work. People hold within them infinite solutions to everyday problems and by watching how they interact with the world you may find things that you want to incorporate or at least try out. More than anything, the master move here is to learn from the mistakes of others. Most people don't learn from their own mistakes, so this is considered an advanced technique. The simplest example of this is walking behind someone on a sidewalk and watching them slip on an icy patch. If you slip in the same place and hurt yourself... you deserved it.

Unlike logical reasoning, people-watching can easily be explained by shorter examples. That simplicity doesn't make it any less effective as a method of streamlining your life. It can be as simple as being at a party and watching someone mix a drink that you have never tried before. You have the choice to either watch closely and try to copy them or use it as an opening to engage them in conversation and try one for yourself. Now you have a new friend/love interest and you know how to make a tasty new drink. Double stress relief.

How about going to the gym, This can be a daunting task for some people; there are so many avenues of fitness and so many ways and programs to try out in the gym before you find what is right for you. It may take years. In the meantime, look around you. Look at the people that have the physique that you desire for yourself. Don't get too caught up on looks but if you notice someone, look at their workout. Gym goers are pumped full of natural endorphins, if they are at all approachable people, anywhere, they are doubly so at the gym or post workout. If someone does an interesting routine that you want to find out more about, just ask them. You can simply observe and research but try not to be too leery about it.

This method also has the effect of helping you to stay motivated, to know what is possible to achieve and see what it takes to get there. Over time you will build a routine that suits your body style, genetics, preferences and desires based on snippets that you have gleaned from other people's workouts. Hopefully you have met a friend or two at the gym as well. This helps the motivation as well, since they will probably call you out on your missed days.

Now onto the most important aspect of people-watching: free relationship advice.

Many strong couples count among their favourite hobbies, people-watching. This method takes many forms. Go and get a hot beverage together in an outdoor patio and watch people passing through. Go to the Mall. Go to a nice restaurant and along with your conversation, keep an ear out for the conversations of others. Go to a dance club. Observe other couples in vehicles in traffic. House parties, dinner parties and games nights are great for this also.

All of these scenarios and more allow you or you and your significant other to detach yourselves from the world you live in and simply observe other people. You get to see old men holding car doors open for their wives. You get to see first hand the reactions that assholes get from their spouses (male or female). You get to observe people on their best and worst behaviour and if you're smart, you can learn from that and avoid the stress of making the same mistakes yourself.

Now, onto the underrated date movie. These all feature the same set up, knock down and recover phases or acts. Act I shows you a couple or would-be couple, but there is one simple thing, one of them isn't doing right. It could be that one of them lies or cheats or spends too much time at work or ignores the kids, you name it. Then, in Act II is where that trait comes to a head and the relationship is in question, the offending person often hits rock bottom. In Act III the person admits and corrects his or her error and is forgiven and they live happily ever after.

As a couple if you watch one of these movies from time to time, it may illuminate an undesirable trait and offers it up for discussion. "Dear, do you feel that I am like the person from the movie?" If that movie can help you to realize that you are not pulling your weight or helps you bring up the fact that your partner isn't pulling their weight, that is a huge ball of stress and anger that you have avoided by detaching yourselves from your lives in an appropriate way to look at the lives of these make-believe people.

Travel and world news can also bring a global aspect to your people-watching. The goal is to be informed from as many sources as possible.

There are multitudes of multifaceted options when we are looking to improve ourselves, if we open our minds and are willing to be taught.

Asking for help

This concept is a way to let go, that is easier for some people than others. What comes to mind is the stereotypical "man of jokes" who won't ask for directions or admit being lost. That is a great example of someone whose head is full. In order to have an open mind and accept new ideas (scary part coming) we sometimes need to admit that we are wrong, or at least that we don't have all the answers. That means we have to put our adult pants on and use our adult voice and that can hurt our egos. We have covered that challenging your ego is actually a good thing, as your ego is not your ally. In the long run we are better served by making a new acquaintance and getting a helping hand to learn the way.

If you see one of those quintessential older couples that have been together for 50+ years. Don't be shy to congratulate them on their love and ask if they have any simple advice to help out a younger couple, or a new parent. Some of that advice may need to be taken with a grain of salt as their marriage happened in a very different time in our world.

If you are struggling with and stressing out about some school work, ask your teacher, or a student who is doing well, you can even hire a tutor to get you through that tough spot. Then be at peace again and ready to soak in the next gem of information.

How is this part of appropriate detachment you ask? How is it letting go? This is a big step, and can be difficult, you need to let go of the idea of yourself as someone who will never need help. Life can be amazing and beautiful but it can also be taxing and complicated and the most important thing to remember is, we are not in it alone. There are people struggling through the same problems you have and within this global community there is probably a web presence or forum of like-minded people with whom you can find solace.

This process can be as simple as getting some friends to help you move or as complicated as doing online research to help you learn how to Thevenize an electronic circuit. You can struggle alone for hours longer and maybe solve it on your own or you can be a bit more humble and ask for help. Solve the problem in a quarter of the time, using that extra free time to accomplish the next challenge.

Detach yourself from your ego and ask for help from time to time.

Help Others

Not to get all "touchy feely" and "change the world" on you but there is a personal benefit from helping others as well. We just covered the freedom of asking for help. You may find your friends and colleagues a lot more interested in helping you if you have helped them at some point. You don't always have to wait for them to come out and ask for it as well.

This idea doesn't have to be all that complicated or revolutionary; it starts pretty simply with the basics of holding doors open for people. This courtesy seems to have lost popularity of late but it goes a long way to helping someone feel like you are aware of them and looking out for them. This can really help lower the stress level of someone who is feeling lonely. Lowering the stress level of people around you is a great way to bring down the stress that is being applied to you in the first place.

So at this point you're probably wondering how does this fit into the "how do you let go?" chapter. We have a tendency to plan out our lives to the minute and schedule our days full of personal tasks. If a friend or family member calls you needing help with something, it may not fit into your current fastidious schedule. That means that we need to decide if we have the energy to help this person but we also need to be generous with our time and perhaps drop something that we had already planned.

It can be difficult to assess the importance of one of your own tasks compared to something a friend needs and prioritize which should be pursued, but that is another aspect of letting go. In time you may find that it isn't necessary to pre-book your schedule so air-tight and the best experiences are often ones that weren't planned. Getting overly trapped in a routine will greatly reduce your number of new experiences which is akin to having a closed mind. Leave room in your schedule for adventure.

There is also the added bonus that you will learn from the outcome of the task you helped with. Help a friend move and you will learn how to pack more efficiently, help a friend with a financial jam and you will learn what to be prepared for, help look after a child or dog and you will learn what it is like to share your life with another creature. Just like before, learn from your surroundings and be a more balanced person.

Simple charitable donation can also be a way to take the "help others" concept to a global scale. The quality of life throughout our globe fluctuates greatly and it may help you feel more at ease to know that you are doing your part to help others.

Be the person that your friends can call at 2AM with a problem, you may find that you foster deeper connections, with a larger group, of interesting people.

The value of other people's opinions of you

Being concerned about other people's perceived opinion of you is a rabbit hole leading to stress and anxiety. Unless that person is your immediate supervisor who is about to write a review that a promotion hangs on, or a potential love interest, you would be amazed at how unimportant their opinion of you actually is to your life.

We spend so much time and energy trying to figure out what someone thinks of us, or trying to impress people. Here is the twist of fate, the less we care about what people think about us, the more highly people will think of us. It sounds counterintuitive but that is the way it works. Think about someone who is aloof and sort of stereotypically "cool", they are relaxed in almost every situation and they don't care what people think about them. Now try to think of someone you know who is a little bit more anxious and worries about what people think of them all the time. It gives off an odd vibe, like that person is hiding their true nature just to fit in. This forces the outside world to fill in the blanks and try to figure out what the person is hiding. What people imagine is often far worse than the truth.

So wait, one chapter says to be physically fit and eat healthy, one of the benefits being that you will look more desirable to your potential fiends and mates, while another chapter says not to care what people think about you. The goal of the health and fitness part is primarily one of personal benefit. The added energy and ability will serve you in all your other endeavours. A byproduct of that work is that you may find people treating you differently or looking at you differently. The goal of not worrying about other people's opinions is also made more attainable when those opinions have a more positive baseline.

Imagine being able to walk into a room at a conference or house party and not be concerned about what new people at the event might think of you. Imagine how much stronger and more memorable a first impression you will make without all that anxiety. That is the power of letting go.

Analyzing potential effect

The concept that we have control over certain aspects of our lives and no control over others isn't a cut and dried line. There are grey areas in between. Most commonly there are things that we have control over up to a certain point. This point of diminishing returns is when you need to decide if it is still efficient to focus your time and energy onto that task or move on to the next thing.

Finding that point can be complex and we will cover it in more detail in a further chapter but it is important to attempt to predict how much, if any, impact we will be able to have over a desired outcome. This task is a bit of a culmination of the methods discussed in this chapter.

Use everything in your experience from living your own life, observing the lives of others and asking for help from others. Add into the mix the life experience gleaned from when you help others and apply logical reasoning to decide how much impact you will have on the desired outcome. This process will help you prioritize your tasks, but more than anything, it will help you figure out which things you can just let go of.

Actually letting go

All of this analysis and divining which tasks to work on and which tasks will continue to progress without you is fine. Actually being able to let go of something which you deem important is a whole other animal. This will be the hardest part and for some, at first, it may even cause you more stress. The concept of looking at a goal or outcome that you value as important and realizing that you can do little to affect the result is already a part of our lives. There is even a coined term for it: "the ball is in their court". This phrase hinges upon a realization that you have no control over the outcome. Embracing that fact and simply detaching yourself from the situation is a bit more foreign.

This is the goal of the journey set out before you, the pay-off is clear but where the path leads you will be your own adventure. How far you go and how fast you get there, will also be completely up to you.

Other systems of belief refer to a similar concept of "faith" but here you are not being asked to commit to something quite so open-ended. Once you discover something that you know is out of your hands, put it out of your mind as well.

6 HOW DO YOU APPLY THIS TO YOUR LIFE?

You have been presented with a fascinating concept and a lot of scenarios about the potential greatness that is just around the corner: the idea of the freedom gained by just letting go. You have seen some great methods for analyzing things in your life and figuring out if they are something you can control or something that can be let go of. The question still remains: "how does it all come together?"

We are going to break down our daily lives into subsections, quickly cover each one and maybe give an example or two of how this concept fits in and what the potential benefits are.

Home-Life
Working our way through a normal day, this is where it all starts. With less worry on the mind, hopefully you will

have just completed a restful night's sleep and now it is time to get ready for the day. A big portion of the home life component is setting up your routine so that you don't add stress where it need not be. This for most people includes mornings. Another adage comes up here: "Do today's work today". When tomorrow arrives there will be a whole new set of tasks that need completing and you won't have time to recover from the tasks you didn't finish today.

This concept can be taken a step further, once you are comfortable completing today's work today, see if you can get a head start on tomorrow. Baby steps at first, if you bring a lunch to work (and you should so that you know what you are eating) make it the night before. Depending on if you are a night person or a morning person you can even shower the night before, pick out your clothes, take out/thaw whatever you need for tomorrow's supper and do some quick stretches before bed.

All this work means being able to wake up first thing in the morning and not having to worry about getting everything ready for the day. Think how much more relaxed your mornings would be if your lunch was already made, your clothes were ready to go and you had a great night's sleep.

There are of course other aspects of home life besides first thing in the morning, but this method will help you prioritize and organize all of them to ensure you are running an efficient household. Setting up a routine for household cleaning will not only help keep the house looking tidy, it will help you be able to find persistently lost items. Regular cleaning has the added benefit of opening your door to a clean house every time you come home. Seeing that mess when you come home only serves to remind you of yet another task that needs to be completed, adding more stress.

Work-Life

While your home-life is perhaps the most important, it is your work life where you will most likely see the largest benefit from appropriate detachment. In time, it will grant you the ability to process and juggle more information, tasks and relationships. Additionally, you will be amazed at how much you can actually accomplish in one day once your mind is free of unnecessary stress.

Applying the same principles that will allow you to streamline the rest of your life, you will find your attitude at work is much more balanced and flexible. Added stress and escalating timetables will have less effect on your brain's ability to simply do the job. Imagine a more staunch reaction to rising stress levels in the workplace. Imagine being the person that is able to save the project by keeping a cool head when the pressure is on.

That all sounds great, but how do you do it? The key here is really no different than any other sphere of life. In your head, or on paper if you must, lay out all of the tasks being asked of you. Try asking this question: "What would happen if this did not get done today?". If the answer is "nothing", then maybe "nothing" is what you should do about that task. Figure out which task will either be due first or have the greatest immediate importance and attack that task with your whole mind.

We have covered the importance of asking for help; nowhere is it more important than your work life. When you have laid out all of your tasks and looked at a realistic timetable and you see absolutely no solution, ask for help. Become a collaborator on projects that need collaboration. Provide opportunities to those around you and below you to shine on tasks that have been assigned to you. This benefits the whole company and ensures that people will be willing to help you, the next time you need it.

That being said, if your timetable has an opening, be open to the idea of helping others with their tasks. Getting credit for helping them is less important, either way you have banked a favour for when you next need their help.

Don't think we left out people-watching — it has an excellent application here as well. If you see a colleague get denied for a proposal, offer to help them correct the proposal. This way you will learn the specifics of why it was denied in the first place. When it is time for you to draft a proposal of your own, you will have gained the experience from their work. If your colleague's proposal is accepted, looking at it will give you a functional template for something that you may need to write in the future.

The work-life benefits from appropriate detachment are legion. You will see progress here quickly, even in the early days of adopting this new concept.

Love-Life

Your love-life is something that can bring you a lot of peace and balance but, if it is unsatisfying or left unfulfilled then it can be a major source of stress and anxiety. Even while in a committed relationship, your love life can fluctuate and your mood and stress level will be directly proportionate. Love life, in this case, doesn't specifically refer to sex but rather affection as a whole. However if you are receiving a good level of overall affection but are still missing a specific outlet, it can still be stressful.

So how does Appropriate Detachment fit into love-life and how does it make things better? The key point is that it will help you to be more tolerant and more open-minded. Realize that in a committed relationship, you are side by side with another real human being, living a life of their own, with desires, needs and boundaries of their own. You need to be able to communicate your needs and be receptive and accommodating of theirs. One and one don't make one or even the more mathematically correct two. 1 and 1 make 11. Two "1" standing side by side, supporting each other and sharing adventures but always being separate people. Looking more deeply, we learn about complimentary opposites — Yin and Yang, each having a spot of the other's colour. This is the ideal pairing, people from two walks of life with things they can do and enjoy together, as well as things they do apart from each other.

With that realization in mind we can start to figure out

all sorts of things for ourselves. Let's start with the hot topic that can make or break a marriage, or simply cause stress, sex. There are all sorts of weird and wonderful ways that two people (or more) can get together and bring pleasure to each other. You may come from a starting point of a specific religious view on the "carnal acts" but in the end, they are a part of life and they create life, some of them anyways.

Logical reasoning dictates that if we do what we can to bring pleasure to our significant other, then they will be more inclined to do what they can, to bring us pleasure. This reciprocal concept, done in a respectful environment, can lead to a very fulfilling love life and a surprisingly close bond, due to mutually shared experiences. Here comes a scary topic for some people; people-watching in this specific case translates to (your mind is there before your eyes are) pornography. This topic is a deal breaker for many people but in truth can be a treasure trove of new ideas that can be gently introduced into the bedroom; Leading you both down a journey of sexual exploration that may bring you to the strongest place your relationship has even been.

So, having an open mind about things will help keep your partner satisfied but there is still the aspect of tolerance. Here is the question you need to ask yourself, much like with diet and nutrition: How much sex does a person really need and am I making unrealistic demands of my spouse? Over time and with good communication you should be able to work out a decent routine that keeps everyone feeling happy and loved, while not feeling sore and used.

Social life

Depending on our personality traits (introverted or extroverted and everything in between) we have differing needs when it comes to social activity. Human nature leans towards social behaviour and now thanks to the internet that can be accomplished without leaving a darkened basement. The end result of Appropriate Detachment on your social life will be to ease off some of the anxiety and stress involved with trying to make such a good impression on people.

Logical reasoning tells us that other people's opinions of us are of fairly low consequence in the grand scheme of things. We also know that not all social interaction is face-to-face, there is much to be said about your web presence. Don't fool yourself into thinking it isn't important. Potential employers, love interests and new acquaintances alike can readily look you up and learn quite a bit about you. What does your online presence say about you?

People-watching is invaluable in unfamiliar social settings. The ability to read a room or cater your conversation to match your audience will have an immeasurable impact on your social graces. Given the chance, take a step back and truly observe the environment, watch people introduce themselves and you will see which ones have gone well and which have left a poor impression. This knowledge will inform your actions to maximize your enjoyment of the time you have committed to this social outing.

Asking for help can be as simple as asking to be introduced to someone that you would like to meet. Offering your help can be small acts of kindness. Opening a door, taking someone's coat, telling someone they have something in their teeth (discretely) or calling someone a cab if they have had too much to drink.

Appropriate Detachment has direct applications to so many aspects of our lives that listing them all would be an exercise in futility. We will however, carry on with a short list of examples to get the proverbial ball rolling.

Parental life

As a parent, especially of young kids or teenagers it can be difficult to find any remaining scraps of energy or mental focus to accomplish other things in your life. Appropriate Detachment will help you remain calm and balanced in the midst of some of the crazy adventures that parenthood can bring.

Let's start with the basics, the patience game. This starts in very early life with a child crying for attention or a perceived want, they then wait to see how long it takes you to react. Over time this evolves to asking for toys or chocolate bars in stores and still later asking for money and car keys. Success or failure on this front is measured by how well your child accepts you saying "no" to something. We are not talking about denying or neglecting the child but instead teaching them to be self-sufficient and to realize that you don't always get what you want, when you want it.

If you can tune out and detach yourself from the complaints at an early age, it will toughen you in terms of caving to their demands. Logical reasoning teaches us to break down our interactions with people and see the causality behind situations.

If your child asks you for a chocolate bar in a store line-up and you say no, stick to your guns, that way the message they receive is: I didn't get a chocolate bar this time but I will try to ask again next time we are here.

If your child begs and pleads and after 5 or even 10 minutes in line you cave and get them one, the message they receive is: as long as I beg long enough I will get what I want. So now you're going to hear it everywhere you go and that is going to add to your stress, anxiety and embarrassment. You have all heard those children in line and you can't help but look at the parent. Imagine all those eyes on you.

A good system might be, if your child wants something, ask them to explain a logical reason for wanting that item and specify why it should be bought today. That method causes them to use their brain and develop useful reasoning skills that will serve them in every aspect of life. "I want it because I want it" or "my friends have one" doesn't cut it.

That is a small example but it illustrates the point, let's explore one final example then move on from parental life. Applying Appropriate Detachment to your parenting could take volumes of books to cover but the key is to give you the tools and allow you to decide how to best apply them to your life. The other point we should cover is raising your voice, getting angry or showing emotion in your voice.

Children can be the most enriching part of our lives but it can also quickly feel like an "us versus them" situation, where we have to compete against our own children for household supremacy.   It can be a psychological battlefield at times, so use your years of experience and wisdom to your advantage, because you are not going to beat them at their own game. You are not going to yell louder than a child or for longer. It is no longer proper to get physical with your children and for good reason: we are massive compared to a small child, there is no contest there and that doesn't prove anything. What is left then? We have evolved enough as a society and as people to be able to use our minds and logical reasoning to work out how to interact with our own children.

If you get angry easily and frequently yell at your children then when something really important happens and you need them to listen right away, it doesn't give you anywhere to go from there. You can't turn your voice up to eleven. But if you are someone who can remain calm and keep your voice and emotions in check, then when you do have to speak up, you may be amazed at the reaction. Without the fear of your temper, you may also find that your children are more willing to bring you their questions and concerns about the stages of life they are going through. Talk to your kids, it is better that they hear these things from you. Think of the alternative.

School life

This book is being written, as much as possible, to cater to a wide audience, from young people in secondary school right through to retirees dealing with changes in life. There should therefore be a reference to life in school. This could relate to junior high, high school, college/university or even short courses that you get sent to from work or at a community center.

The core concept of being a student is to absorb knowledge, to learn. The empty cup principal is integral in the ability to learn new information. If you are sure that you know something, you won't be receptive to learn anything new about it. With an open, humble mind you can learn much faster as you avoid the concept of comparative learning. This concept happens when you get a new nugget of information and you are forced to check that nugget against everything your mind already knows to see if there are any conflicts before tentatively accepting it as something learned. Even then it will sit on a virtual maybe pile, in case something new comes along and conflicts with it.

Embrace conflicting information — that is when you actually get to use your brain. This comes back to complimentary opposites and allows us to avoid something that plagues this world. The concept of singular truth. The belief goes like this: "If I believe ____ to be true, and I am not wrong, then anyone with a different opinion must be wrong". This is a scary fundamentalist mindset and needs to be discouraged everywhere but in mathematics. Even there, the end result of an equation has a fixed answer but there are many ways to get there. Many questions have a multitude of correct answers and it is only by exploring all of the possible answers that we will ever truly understand the question.

Yet another great definition of fundamentalism is when we lose our sense of humour about something. If you can't laugh at a well-crafted joke about something then you are in it too deep.

Another great benefit that Appropriate Detachment will afford any student is the ability to tune out everything outside of the classroom. High school can be a very scary place, full of bullies and cliques and all sorts of insecurities and that can seem soul-crushing, as if life itself may end. It is important for any high school student to know just how little consequence that stuff will have on your adult life. The ability to realize that and tune out as much as possible of that stress while in class, will free up your mind to truly absorb the material, which will lead you down a path to success. If you apply yourself enough to the things that actually matter, your success is essentially guaranteed.

Play-life

You can't live your life in work mode all of the time. Even if you love your job and it is very fulfilling you still need to strike a balance in life or the lack of variety will slowly eat at you. The play aspect of your life (at any age) is vitally important to your health, both physically and mentally. This idea doesn't necessarily refer to throwing a ball around or building something with plastic blocks, but it could mean that.

Find a hobby or pastime that you enjoy and take some time on a regular basis to indulge in it. If you are in a committed relationship it would be courteous to consider the schedule of your spouse and/or children when planning this activity and be sure to allot them the needed time to indulge in a similar outlet. If the outlet you choose is something that can be done in the house, then perhaps a good time for it might be when others are asleep. For many couples, one person is an early riser and one may go to bed a little later, allowing each to have some solo time to engage their chosen hobby.

In relationships it is often beneficial to have things that you enjoy doing together but it is also important to have things you like to do apart. You need to have that time away or with friends to get some space and develop new stories to share with your significant other.

For the sake of an example let's use golf as a potential hobby. Golf allows for exercise (although not particularly vigorous exercise) and gets you outside, in the sun, enjoying the scenery. It allows for up to four friends to spend 4-5 hours applying themselves to a puzzle that requires fine control of the whole body. While you are away playing golf, you are building up new stories and at the same time getting a respite from your home life. Even if your home life is great, a break for the sake of variety can do a lot of good.

While you are playing golf, your spouse is now free to do whatever it is they like to do, some solo time with a book, a video game, watch a movie you aren't into, go out with their friends or simply nap.

While we are on the subject, video games have quite an awful stigma in the media and in certain circles of society. Anything that improves your ability to use a computer, navigate complex unfamiliar menus, think your way through puzzles and improve you eye-hand coordination and manual dexterity can't be a complete waste of time. There are surgeons who swear their life-saving hand skills were honed playing flight simulator games with a joystick. There are writers who were inspired by a story line they saw in a game. A whole generation has been inspired through video games by the creative power of computers and sought out new jobs that expand our understanding of what they are capable of.

Appropriate Detachment allows you to clear your mind of social stigma, along with a myriad of imposed deterrents. Women can lift heavy weights at the gym, Men can do Yoga and Pilates, and 70-year-old retirees as well as 12-year-old boys can play video games. There is a whole world of adventure and fun to be had and more hobbies than can be easily named. All with global communities, getting together online and collaborating. Find one or more that suit you and join in on the fun.

Creative-life

While we are on the topic of finding something that suits your interests and getting some enjoyment out of it, most people find it beneficial to have a creative outlet in their lives. This can tie in with one of your hobbies or for some; it can be a hobby or passion in itself. Once again there are many options, allowing you to find something to your liking.

Some people paint, some draw, some sing or play an instrument, sewing, knitting, crochet, home improvement, heck some people even write philosophy/self-help books...

Having a place to channel your creative energies can be a wonderful way to get them out of your head and onto a piece of paper or fabric, freeing room in your brain for the next thing it needs to do. Truly finding the right creative outlet can also be incredibly therapeutic.

You don't need to be creating your magnum opus or painting a masterpiece right out of the gate, but you won't know what you are capable of unless you try it. Start small, write in a journal or simply complete a crossword or sudoku puzzle. The last two examples don't allow for unique creation but at least there is something on the page that wasn't there when you started and that may spark something for you.

So we have learned that having a creative outlet can benefit our lives. Now on to how Appropriate Detachment can benefit our creative outlets. Have you ever tried to write a story or a poem with people talking loudly in the room? Have you ever tried to compose music while someone else is watching TV in the room? How about drawing a picture while someone is constantly trying to get your attention? The key to creativity is focus. Athletes call it being "in the zone".

Sometimes chaos spurs focus, so don't rule it out. Fast music at the gym or while drawing can speed up your mind. If the music is faster than your mind can process, then your brain will perk up but not be able to focus on the music and therefore just sort of drift. The electronica version is referred to as "trance" music and this is perhaps a fitting name. Certain religions and philosophies speak of meditation and stillness to block out the world around you and allow you to focus your whole being on a primary task.

There is no fast track to inner focus and mental oneness but there are a few things you can do to get the journey started. The Buddhists believe in doing away with all desires until the only desire left is a life without desires. That way in the end you only have one thing to drop and then you are free. This speaks to eliminating distractions. Appropriate Detachment erodes away your reliance on minor status updates from tasks that are out of your control, allowing you to live your life less distractedly. Nowhere is that more important than in your creative pursuits.

You may find that music, played on good quality headphones, will block out most of the distractions of the world. The right music however, must be found for the right task. If you intend on writing something then maybe don't chose overly lyrical music. Movie and video game soundtrack music is designed to perk up your brain without stealing your attention that sounds like what we want. If you are painting a happy picture, maybe avoid any music in a minor key. In time you may find that you can block out the world and quiet your mind without the music. Don't try to eliminate all the little noises and distractions, one at a time. Block them all out with the music and when you feel ready, let the music go as well. You may find that those initial distractions don't bother you any more, like the Buddhist being set free by letting go of the final desire.

Financial-life

Now we come to the great divider, the cause of the majority of marital spats and one of the strongest sources of stress in modern life, money. How much is "enough"? There are A-list, blockbuster actors who have a penchant for buying islands and mansions and therefore run out of money despite multi-million dollar movies deals. There are janitors who make an inconceivable fraction of that money and are satisfied with what they have and live happily.

So what is "enough" then? It's all in our heads. In your work life, if you chase money rather than a job you truly enjoy, then you will always be miserable. If you find a job you truly love, then you may find yourself excelling at it and you may be surprised by where that takes you financially. The suggestion here is not that money is the "root of all evil". You are not being discouraged to make money. Create a life that you enjoy and are happy with and then see where the money comes from.

When it comes to money and if we are making

"enough" we are often our own worst enemy. We either copy the desires of other people or try to compete with them in terms of possessions or vacations. Traveling the world is a good thing; you need some perspective on how other people live their lives. You won't gain perspective from a beach in Cuba, a resort in Jamaica or a casino in Vegas. You need to visit the real world if you wish to return home having learned anything, not some small area artificially designed to be like a storybook.

If you consistently chose to simply go on escape vacations and do so quite often, ask yourself this: Why not build a life that you don't continuously feel the need to escape from?

Through Appropriate Detachment you can better prioritize the money you currently make, to ensure it provides you with the things that are most important to you. Use logical reasoning and create a simple budgetary spreadsheet to find out where all of that money actually goes. Track your spending over a sample period of time and analyze your lifestyle to decide if what you are buying is truly needed. You might be amazed at how much money is wasted on incidentals.

Making yourself a luxury coffee or Tea at work or at home will rarely cost you more than a dollar. Many people pay more than four dollars every day in a shop, sometimes getting more than one per day. That can add up in a hurry. Let's say the difference is three dollars, over a month that is $90, $1080 on the year. Think about where that money could go to reduce stress and alleviate anxiety. Pay off a debt that is bothering you, or support a new hobby or creative output.

You are in control of your financial life and it is time that you realize that and stop playing the victim. It is your life and your money; you decide where it goes and when it is gone, it is gone. If you lay out everything that you spend money on and focus a larger portion of money to the things that you deem more important and slowly erode away the money going to the less important items you will find yourself living a more rewarding, less stressful life.

Conclusion

This chapter barely scratches the surface of the applications of Appropriate Detachment to your day-to-day life. Our lives are all so diverse that we could never plan for every eventuality. The beauty of this philosophy is that it starts you on a journey that will be shorter for some and won't always lead to the same destination. Armed with the right tools to evaluate your situation and react to whatever may come, it can be quite an adventure.

Where will the journey take you?

7 PRIORITIZING WHERE YOU CAN MAKE THE BIGGEST IMPACT

Aspects of our life are rarely completely out of our control or fully under our control. It is then up to us to determine where in life we can best apply our finite energy and brainpower, to make the greatest impact.

To begin with, it may be easier to lay out everything that you think needs doing on a sheet of paper or on a computer. Set up two columns of numbers. In the first, rank the tasks by the priority you feel the task deserves; this can be based on how soon it needs to be completed or how bad the fallout would be if it failed. In the second column, rank them by how responsible you are for the completion of that task. Your number one item, in column two, should be something that you must do and you can't possibly get any help with or maybe you can't even talk to someone about for advice; something that is fully your responsibility.

When you see these tasks all laid out, you may begin to see patterns and correlations that will help you better prioritize your time and energy. The sooner you complete a reasonable portion of these tasks, the sooner you can move on to some play or creative time.

In time you may find you are able to keep track of a good portion of this list in your head and juggle the priorities on the fly. Minute changes in your life can greatly impact the order of things on this list, or bring in whole new topics. Therefore try not to let the maintenance of this list become yet another task on it. This is a tool to help you decide where to act, don't let it take over.

Let's take a moment to cover the making of lists. Some people are addicted to making lists. For some, this is a needed process to help them visualize what needs to be done. The danger of too many lists is that after a while, they just become itemized reminders of work you still need to do. That can overwhelm, and build up until it seems impossible to escape them. Make sure that the time you spend making lists isn't what is keeping you from actually accomplishing the tasks on them.

So we have covered the idea that if you have absolutely no control over something, the best course of action is to simply let it go and detach yourself from it. Now we take a tiny step into the grey area from there. Imagine a task that is in someone else's hands but if we really lay out every eventuality, there is something we can do. It will require an enormous effort on our part with very little effect and in some cases may even backfire or make us seem desperate. Does that sound like an effective use of energy?

Let's walk through that idea with a scenario. Let's say you are competing at work with three other people for a promotion. The decision is in your supervisor's hands and the reporting period for the work that he or she is evaluating has already passed. At this point, although it is something very important to you, the task belongs to your supervisor, you have already done your part.

If you want to get specific about it, you could sniff around for gossip to find out who the other three people are. You could try to do something to discredit them in the eyes of the supervisor, and this does happen, all too often. As often as not though, devious schemes tend to backfire and illuminate the true nature of their plotter. You could try to kiss-up to your supervisor, bringing in coffee and sweets, offloading some of their work or simply being overly polite to them. An experienced supervisor can see right through that; some will love the attention and some will see it for what it is, a mark on your character.

You would be best served by putting the idea of the promotion out of your mind and simply moving on with your work life. Focus on a project that needs your attention and you will prove yourself to be the person they are looking for: A dedicated, cool-minded worker that knows when it is important to complete a task.

Stress accumulates when we don't feel we have the

time, skill or energy to complete all of the tasks that have been assigned to us. Appropriate Detachment helps us realize which tasks we should tackle first and allows us to focus on them with our whole being. Without the distractions of other tasks roaming around in our mind we can be so much more productive. Just let them go.

8 WILL THIS MAKE ME AN EMOTIONLESS ROBOT?

This all sounds well and good but there seems to be a danger in detaching ourselves from our emotions. If everyday you have a good day, you are never mad or stressed or overly tired, does that mean you are somehow less human?

To an outside eye, seeing someone who can weather disappointment and bounce back from a hardship may seem somewhat askew. Inspire them, show them how resilient and productive a human being can really be. Too many people use the word "human" as an excuse, "I'm only human..." Let's redefine that term, rather than hide behind it.

We must be very clear here, there is a dangerous difference between bottling up your emotions and detaching yourself from the sway they have on your decision-making process. Bottling up anything besides wine and scotch is a bad idea. The goal is to be empty, so that we are ready to receive new information, new experiences, and truly live. You can't do that if you are still filled with rage or hurt or scorn from the last experience. Just let it go, it isn't helping anyone.

If someone comes by and asks you "You always seems so calm, no matter what is going on, how do you do it?" tell them, spread the word.

9 SPREADING CALM INTO THE WORLD

Think of it as de-escalation. You understand the concept of escalation: person 1 yells at person 2, so 2 hits him, so 1 gets a stick, 2 gets a knife, 1 gets a gun, 2 gets a tank, 1 gets a plane, bomb, nuke, so on... what is left in the end? Do we even remember why we were fighting? This "solution" solves nothing. Gandhi said "Be the change you want to see in the world". This book is not heavy on quotes although many inspire it. That singular quote is important enough to be included right in the text. Be the change.

Christians refer to "turning the other cheek" and if you are a Christian and you want to link these concepts, that works great. This philosophy however is open to all religions and even people who don't prescribe to a predefined system of thought.

This concept is universal; the world isn't going to

magically become a less stressful place for you to live in, just because you asked it to. You have to make the change in your life. The people that you interact with will inevitably notice this change in you. They will notice how calm you are, how in control, and more than anything how effective you are at using your time and energy. They will ask about it or comment on it, don't be shy and don't hoard your wisdom. Let them know about Appropriate Detachment, lend them a copy of the book, buy it for someone as a gift, get the word out there. You may even feel comfortable enough to help guide someone through the early stages.

Remember that you are not going to be a Zen Master right away and that it is important to apply moderation to all things in your life. If you ease your way into Appropriate Detachment you will find it more palatable and you may even have fewer snags along the way.

Let's work out the logical reasoning of the benefits of sharing this information. Imagine a workplace where your whole team is calm and collaborative. No one wastes time or spins their wheels because they are afraid of asking for help and everyone focuses their whole being towards completing a mutual project. Can you even fathom what you would be capable of as a true team?

Imagine a family life where no one explodes and yells at anyone else without legitimate reason. A parental life where you can freely and openly talk to your kids and they feel comfortable openly talking to you.

Imagine a school life where all of your classmates are focused on learning and no one wastes energy with bullying and put-downs.

Imagine a world full of calm people that analyze their environment and decide on the best course of action, rather than making snap reactions based on hatred and greed. Imagine what we can accomplish as a collaborative whole. What could we accomplish if we stopped opposing each other and instead focused that energy on working together?

What indeed?

ABOUT THE AUTHOR

Drew Torchia is an independent Canadian author with an unquenchable thirst for knowledge and wisdom. He has dedicated his life to the study of anything he can get his hands on. In the process, he has amassed lessons and wisdom from many cultures and periods, assembling them into a way of life that streamlines a lot of the complications of modern times.

www.ingramcontent.com/pod-product-compliance
Lightning Source LLC
Chambersburg PA
CBHW070534030426
42337CB00016B/2200